Prairiehead

Prairiehead

poems by

Brian Palmer

© 2023 Brian Palmer. All rights reserved.
This material may not be reproduced in any form, published,
reprinted, recorded, performed, broadcast,
rewritten or redistributed without
the explicit permission of Brian Palmer.
All such actions are strictly prohibited by law.

Cover image "Empty Chairs, Open Door" by Craig Palmer
Author photo by the author

ISBN: 978-1-63980-397-2

Kelsay Books
502 South 1040 East, A-119
American Fork, Utah 84003
Kelsaybooks.com

for Aparna

On we sail—the hills, the sea, the sky. Sail on.

Acknowledgments

Grateful acknowledgment is made to the editors of the following publications in which some of the poems in this collection first appeared, a few in slightly different versions.

Amethyst Review: "To Basho," "Magpie," "On a Northern Shore," "To Be Fed," "To See the Shining Here"

Bristlecone: "I Once Sat by a Sumac in the West," "Yes, Then I'll Go"

The Ekphrastic Review: "The Veteran"

Expansive Poetry Online: "Cranes," "John," "Lyrics," "Sedna's Hands," "Once More Briefly Whole," "Prairiehead," "Peaches in the Growing Orchard," "Sapphic by the Water," "She Is Earth and Sea," "Separation"

The High Window: "the open window brings inside," "Postcards"

The Lyric: "Lines"

Small Framer's Journal: "At This Table," "Each Day and Dusk," "I Am the Alfalfa Farmer"

The Society of Classical Poets: "The Hills and Hours," "Night Verses"

Contents

Prologue

Lyrics   15

I In the Ramshackle Middle of Nowhere

I Once Sat by a Sumac in the West   19
Lines   20
Postcards   21
Magpie   23
Once More Briefly Whole   24
I Am Not Afraid   25
Like Water Falling   26
Winter-quiet   27
Prairiehead   28

II On Humble Soil

I Am the Alfalfa Farmer   31
Each Day and Dusk   32
The Veteran   33
At This Table   34
John   35
To Be Fed   37
Out in February   39

III Hearts in the West

She Is Earth and Sea   43
Sapphic by the Water   44
For an Orchid   45
India on the Phone, Aubade and Serenade   46
Separation   49
Sedna's Hands   50
the open window brings inside   52

IV Still

Yes, Then I'll Go	55
On a Northern Shore	56
To Basho	57
Already	58
To See the Shining Here	59
The Hills and Hours	60
Cranes	61
Night Verses	62

Prologue

Lyrics

They float in yards, in fields, and in wild places, too,
The pipe-notes, all day long, and just within our earshot;
Lyrics are the air, wood, water, rocks, and rain.

In scores, set free, they mingle in the shade of peach,
Beneath the osier, rose, and beech, and some rise sunward
Over foxes trotting through fresh fallen snow.

And when we're close to sleep, they come to light on us.
We touch our fingertips so sure that vague impressions
From those ancient instruments still linger there.

We are bound—not mired in ash piles at our feet—
To follow life to shady green remembered sounds;
Lyrics are the air, wood, water, rocks, and rain.

I
In the Ramshackle Middle of Nowhere

I Once Sat by a Sumac in the West

I once sat by a sumac in the west
insisting to exist in a remote
dry corner at the crux of four fenced fields.

It lived just past a scattered pole corral
behind an empty hay-roofed loafing shed.
Its three-toothed autumn leaves had turned to red.

The memory of that ember-plant revives
in me a spirit that's been sleeping, waking
now as daylight smolders into dusk.

Clear marble dawn will find me flying down
the windy streams of lonely backroads looking
for leaves unfurling green, refiring

the West, that masterwork, enduring even
in the ramshackle middle of nowhere.

Lines

I travel lines of many kinds, some bent, some straight as nails,
moving always parallel to roadsides, rivers, rails

to live a life of words and scenes. I saunter through my days—
backyards, freight yards, up long trails, down hidden alleyways.

I'm unafraid of *nowhere,* rather there is where I find
an emptiness and peacefulness where quiet fills my mind.

No fences need be crossed to eat, thank earth for roaming roots.
And thank tall leaning stalks of grain and wind for windfall fruits.

At noon there's time in forest groves away from human crowds
to gaze through leafy chandeliers at drifting, harmless clouds.

Above hot fields of dusty wheat, the magpies sweep the sky.
They rise and fall with ribbon tails and chuckle as they fly.

The sun sets in the dusky hills and casts long, fiery beams
that turn the land and sky to gold and weary thoughts to dreams.

Sometimes a fragile moon is held in thin black limbs of trees.
It breaks like glass to silver shards with just the slightest breeze.

Mysteries float in between the stars and darkened skies,
like floods in deserts, thirst at sea, and vision without eyes.

One day my feet will meet the point where lines all coalesce;
I'll simply vanish out of view, not more, and nothing less.

Postcards

Morning bright and sunny, then some storms turned up.
Rained hard and soon red water poured from over lips
of canyons, water ladders, water full of gravel,
near, far, high, low. Shushing. Think of locust pods
that we'd collect to shake the seeds in long dry husks—
that's the sound it made but times a thousand. Then the sun
came out. It seemed the rocks and cliffs were washed in nacre.

Noon today was hot and bright. I took a turn
and found myself on some old road with weeds that grew
up through the pavement. I felt lost but found myself.
I parked behind a barn in cool green quiet shade.
Some signage spoke for those who'd made a living there,
then died. I slept with them in light and sighing winds.
I thought I heard your voice, but it was just an owl.

The sky's been wide and blue. I took a rented boat
out on the lake complete with cabins and wood smoke.
I motored easy, slow and safe, and thought of you
with me as small green waves *thunked* on the boat's thin bow.
I cast my line all afternoon and waited for
the tug of fish. I heard wind chimes in slanting light
and made for shore in shadows. Hadn't caught a thing.

These flowers grow on banks of rivers near this place.
And by the way, I'm still amazed that you once fished
those giant northern rivers, what you called "big water,"
eyes filling, flashing in the telling. . . .Well, I'm off.
The weather, maps, and roads all call to unknown places.
I promise, I will not keep time, and not rely
on signs or floods or ghosts or shores to live. I'll try.

Another evening. Sunset view. Coyote clouds
are sailing through, red, yellow, blue. The neon sign
out front reads in the dusk: "THE –AGON WHEEL."
One planet's in the sky already. Perfect. You
should see the store (and diner) down this blacktop road
with bait and fuel and fresh-made pies and cans of beer.
You'll have to come with me sometime. Wish you were here.

Magpie

You line this gift of sky with falling arcs—
up, down, then lower down up again, down—
the form of flight less crucial than the flight

itself. You've not enough resplendent plumes
that might paint green a Guatemalan jungle.
Instead, you sketch the wind with pencil tail.

You look for shade in cottonwoods; in truth,
as stoic in the heat, you shade yourself
and keep your heart eclipsed by your own wings.

On posts, in tangled snags, along thin lines,
in self-silhouette you prophesy nothing
like the returning, bright Quetzalcoatl.

But let me tell you, plain and simple bird:
I long to touch your black and white feathers.

Once More Briefly Whole

It's dawn again and you with earthly senses
make your way across this lonesome prairie,
dodging eyes and slipping under fences,
loping on with backward glances, wary.

Or are you looking for your ardent past
when you, encircled by the face of Moon,
felt bound and loved? By day, you merely cast
a pale companion through the afternoon.

Some solace comes when in relief the walls
of mesas stand a darker black than night,
and Moon in all her phases rises, falls,
with you in thrall to her ephemeral light.

And in those moments, once more briefly whole,
you howl the O of your soon sundered soul.

I Am Not Afraid

I'm not a normal human being, being
who I am, a man who lives forever.

I never lie awake at night and listen
to my heart—it beats and beats and beats.

Reflections in the mirror don't bother me.
My skin and bones will last perpetually.

I'm not compelled to marvel at the fiery
break of days that turn and turn eternally.

Green fields remain in bloom for me, in yellow,
purple, blue, for I forever am.

Fall's first chill is summer still for me,
and autumn's changes never change a thing.

I don't see grace in pure, white-lovely snow,
and never muse, *how brief is snow.* Or Eden.

I do not fear that long and dusky sleep.
I live and breathe. And I am not afraid.

Like Water Falling

Thoughts of wild and timeless falls
rush through me as the seasons run,
as I, this cottonwood, and canyon
change and all so quickly age.

I've wandered down hot shimmering rails,
the straights and curves across the plains.
I've drifted in the shade with sparrows,
whirling like the notes they sang.

I've followed, too, cool glimmering trails:
the Cedar, Cuyahoga, Snake,
the Colorado, Escalante,
Platte, Missouri, and Palouse,

let loose along the way a heart
that's pounding still, still falling from
those young green days through yellow leaves
that in fall-trembling sounds like water

over bone, wood, stone, the rush
of diminishment—
                      here, the tumbling
song of a canyon wren comes to soothe
me at this cliff's red shattered foot.

Winter-quiet

It descends on me as I go up:

a single leaf twists, tapping with small clatter
inside bones, a heart determined, holding fast;

a bird and its own shadow speak—resounding
caws in Wingate halls—of loss and solace;

in faith, cones drop and sigh on snow, content
to lie between the earth and sky till spring;

surrender is the white susurrant stir
of pine and juniper.

                    As clouds accumulate,
and snow falls down on snow, I find that what
descends on me is what I've met half-way:
some part of *leaf, crow, seed,* and *tree* resides
in *me* and echoes true, as by my will
I walk into this winter-quiet day.

Prairiehead

A Midwest train once threw me into rows
of corn. As I lay wounded, grass ingrained
its voice in me. Night wheeled. At dawn, I rose.
Across the miles that sound has long remained.

And now out west at noon, I stand beside
a wind-swept railroad siding when the song
of summer grass again resounds inside
my prairiehead, a whispered tune of long-

stemmed ryegrass waving wild that I on purpose
touch to feel its stalks of seed-heads, stars
on blue, as shadows move across the surface
of the plains like ghosts of passing boxcars.

What outward bears this inward field I know
was planted far from here, and long ago.

II

On Humble Soil

I Am the Alfalfa Farmer

I'm an alfalfa farmer in this world.
In spring I stitch the furrows in my field
straight, long, and deep, heaving up tumbling curled
earth under paper April clouds that shield
sewn seeds from sun which soil, too, keeps concealed
      until green winds come murmuring in May
      when, thin as threads, the dicots rise to day.

I have farmed alfalfa my whole life.
I find peace in swaying purple blooms.
I have a farm, a disc, a truck, a wife
(who loses me in June to fields and rooms
of barns). Late drenched-then-dry July consumes
      me. I must by now have a hay heart.
      It's endless: mowing one day, then the start

of new, young green the next, a sheen of clover;
it grows unceasingly in August haze.
I work until my high hay loft spills over.
I toil with purling turns my field and days
until December comes and winter stays
      the growing season. A calm cold is cast—
      alfalfa, me, in dust, at rest, at last.

Each Day and Dusk

I work inside the fence of my own field.
What lies outside is not my first concern.
Those good, hard chores belong to other men:
Ray's sheep. O'Brien's cattle. Ander's wheat.
Bor, dead, still works beneath his fertile acres.

In rain or sun, I walk a hundred miles
each day, it seems, down rows on humble soil
containing part of me and all my years.

At dusk I turn for home. The wind holds smoke.
The cycle of the full between two sickle
moons is telling of my fruitful life—
the growing, ripening, falling at my hands.

And in the dark, I glean my words like grain,
alone inside a universe of lamplight.

The Veteran

After Winslow Homer's The Veteran in a New Field *(1865)*

In bronzing sun he toils away and swings with smooth broad strokes
his sickle blade made sharp and clean and ready with a stone.
And so it's always been. Perhaps his instruments of war
have changed. With evening's holy care and task of reverence,
he daily fells ripe wheat, not men. Chaff glints in yellow air.

He lives and strives alone beneath his roof and wide-brimmed hat.
When noontime comes he doffs his Union coat and works the land.
The storm that took his brothers' lives yet lingers close at hand,
and mustering clouds of sky's own stores of fierce and fenceless thunder
lurk in dark blue acres, always there to lay men low.

His sun-fired wheat burns harvest red while gray war smolders still.
In scything swaths of tender grain that gathers at his feet,
he hears the hum of distant guns and sighs of dying men.
He wipes his face and drinks his fill and marches through the grass,
and leans and turns his body for the sake of aftermath.

Generals coldly wage and watch their battles from the hills.
Herodotus is watching, too, from hills beyond the frame,
who sees the men, but not as wheat, their blood, but not as rain—
he reaps the truth in all his numbers of the fallen dead,
and dreams of soldier-farmers turning killing fields to bread.

At This Table

A picnic, roadside, at this table
near Montana wheat, in June
still silver-green outlined in black,
he hears the hum and swish of hills.
In noontime winds, the surface moves
like the gesturing skin of cuttlefish.

He sits with knife and cuts his bread
and ponders cryptic, timeless things
while eating flakes of salmon, apples,
food that's watery, salty, sweet—
like memories, and they do come
beneath the blue, in yellow heat.

And so he conjures at this table
far afield at mealtime rest
all those who once had worked the land.
Like his, like him, with lilting voice,
their shadows fly across the lea:
They harvest day. They hear the sea.

John

Rain that fell so hard at dusk is lighter
in the darkness now yet falls still, steadily,
with will, as if to make this night eternal,
turning me to letters to unlock
some higher meaning, finding I'm unable
to escape the thoughts of earthly things.

    His field. The smell of hay, all wet, so pungent. . . .

Such digressions. I should strive for words
about a saint, a convert, the betrayer,
how they suffered on their plains of doubt
and taught me faith beyond myself. Instead,

    I watched the farmer watch the sky and then
    Begin to bale his hay that lay in windrows,
    Trying to outwork the coming storm. . . .

Or maybe I should write of running through
the pouring rain out to a chasm's edge,
of falling, linen then enshrouding me,
my body being lain in soft, green grass
beside the sandaled feet of rose-crowned marble
Mary white against a pure blue sky.

    He failed at last as rain began to fall.
    He left his field, his chore undone—I felt
    His human anguish at that dusky moment. . . .

I sit distracted by the rain, and by
the questions: Could I farm this late in life?
Plant and tend and gather with the hope of finding
answers in the sureness of the seasons?

Tonight, his failure courses through me still.

Who am I in this mysterious world?
I suppose that I am who I am, working
rows of ink to simple, measured lines, like

Soon the sun will rise and dry the earth

and hope they lift above the earth enough
that they might whisper intimations
as the hay, half-harvested, conveys:

That all of us will someday fall again
beneath the scythe of love and leave behind
the rain, the toil, and this infernal night.

To Be Fed

I saw him in the grocery line lay down
a can of beans, a loaf of bread, some milk.
I paid his bill, a total of two dollars.

And now we walk apart in winter twilight,
my dog with me and he alone, our food
in knapsacks—mine, full, yet feels hollow still.

I should have given him my pears, imagining
how round and sweet they would have tasted
in his cardboard lean-to near the river.

I walk past geese out gleaning tattered cornfields.
Measured, ordered, land is parceled, owned.
In their migrations, "in" and "out" are moot;

the remnant fields for them are for surcease,
for the gathering of some meager sustenance,
since they, as do the multitudes, must eat.

In the falling dark and cold their barking builds,
and then they lift, the pull itself ineffable
inside a wild cacophony of calls.

I stop. My dog continues down the road.
As snow begins to fall, I stand and listen
to them fade into the feathery gray.

I turn for home but feel a gnawing hunger
to be desperate in the landscape, too, half-
alive, in search of scattered seeds, of rising

high enough to get my bearings, somewhere,
seeing far below those men—me, him—
the geese, the dog, all looking for a place

to rest our wings and heads and hearts, to eat
our cache of bitter food, to deem ourselves
as beautiful. And finally, to be fed.

Out in February

I leave
myself, the barn,
the lighted yellow-warm,
and walk into the cold
and moonless sea of night, feet cracking through a shell-ice
into snow with cadenced steps
across the windy field
to be alone
inside the
dark.

I stop.
The humbled Queen,
the Dragon, Bear, and King,
spin, anchored to a dim
but certain, pulsing polestar overhead, as spindrift
lifts and wraps my figure in
a fine white crystal coat,
a chrysalis
of winter
rime.

        I weigh an arctic choice:
        to turn to wind and ice,
        or be the animal

I am.
An owl, who stands
up on the hay hood's beak
floats out his feathered word
repeatedly, in layers, each round whole-note telling
me who's left behind. And so,

in hollow tracks made here,
I make my way
in silence
home.

III

Hearts in the West

She Is Earth and Sea

She is dawn, a grayscale figure walking
windswept on a strand of shining pools,
a purple sea star, seagrass, turban snail.
She's crashing waves that rush, splash, cold and fresh.

She is rice on warm tin plates, her life
sustaining lands that ring the Seven Seas.
And me. She's half-moon mango slices. Dal.
Heart, skin, eyes, she's made of earth and India.

And she's the red rock monuments that sail
the rolling swells of sea green desert sage.
A shipwrecked castaway and one who saves
the lost and lonely, she is both of these.

At dusk, a silhouette on red, she gathers
what she loves in bowls of nacred shell:
smooth sea glass shards, like crystal drops of waves,
and urchin bones, etched amulets unbroken.

She is earth and sea, and more to me,
each night and day, the shore and pulse of tides.

Sapphic by the Water

Flowers gather. Rivers are deep and flowing.
Grain stalks rise up firmly in sunlight streaming.
Pathways beckon. Footfalls, soft, lead to shadows.
Love lies beside you.

Voices, quiet; whispers create new verses;
heartbeats, bouquets, music, the scent of springtime:
all a living banquet when someone waits there.
Love lies beside you.

City neon glows here at midnight brightly,
blinding eyes that strive in the dark-hearted
streets of deep desire unrequited, thirsty,
looking for shining

water bearing petals away downstream now.
Freshened bodies sleep in the swaying grasses.
Lucid morning, lightly, once more is breathing.
Love lies beside you.

For an Orchid

I stand behind a veil of wet, new willow limbs
and think of you inside your open-windowed room
where spring comes in, warm pools of moonlight on the floor.

The wind in strings of young green leaves now speaks for me,
low whispered words. You lean to hear, an orchid ear
in misty air; your face is hidden in the curtains.

The moon between the clouds is ringed, and rain-drenched light
drips down on you, now gone to sleep, and me inside
the jeweled willow trembling in the yellow dawn.

India on the Phone, Aubade and Serenade

You, this round and setting moon, are both
in view, just out of reach, and far away.

The Perseids like sudden flaming arrows
burn up soon, so soon, beyond the moon.
I see them in the corner of my eye,
fleeting things, like words that fly from me.

Here in the west, this summer night is filled
with racing cars and laughing girls, dogs, frogs,
and crickets, jangling coins on ice cream counters.
Matches scratch, and insouciant bottle rockets
whistle, arc, and die with feeble snaps.
Screen doors on springs creak open and bounce shut
with family visits, children out past dusk,
neighbors whispering, as sprinklers speak
of gardens, green, complacently of plenty.

I'm sleepy at the open window, holding
on the line, connected as they wake you.
"Hurry! There's a call! The States! From home!"
Their voices echo down the hall, *from home.*
But you're home *there.* It is morning there.
It's tomorrow there.

I wait. My heart, an owl, beats in my night.
Through the phone I hear the sounds of morning
coming through your open-windowed flat:
a single barking dog, the creaking cart
of a lime seller singing in the alley;
the first few frenzied blasts of auto horns;
a high-pitched, tinny voice on the radio
reporting last night's cricket matches;

the flutter of some curtains in a breeze
that must be staving off, for now, the sure,
oppressive heat of the emerging day.
In the rustle of loose posters on the walls,
I hear the whistling rush of Rama's arrows,
the pouring jingle of pure Lakshmi's coins.
I catch the piercing cries of pairing hawks
that twine above the humble temples, binding
up the wounds and ruins of empire.
In stainless-steel rattling from the kitchen,
I taste breakfast of dosa, rasam, sambar,
and endless bowls of mango, crescent slices.

Where am I in your India's rising day?
Perhaps I'm one of those men crowding round
A steaming urn of coffee on a teeming
city corner under towering glass and steel,
or a farmer walking down a country road,
ox cart filled with bright, plump Ooty carrots
to sell at market, lush and jungle hemmed.

Maybe I'm the wild blue bison floating
like a phantom through the singing trees.
A cloud perhaps, above the green Red Hills,
or its shadow on a white-washed shantytown.
Or am I that one lonely figure working
in the tranquil yellow morning haze,
moving down the straight, long hedges
with intermittent, tall white oaks
in silhouette on etched out, terraced land,
picking the top three leaves of *camellias*
to make my daily bundle of strong orange
pekoe tea to carry on my back
at twilight past the boss on the veranda?

No. I'm *here*. It's the moonlit nighttime here.
It's still today, here.

I sit, the seconds drifting in the air,
and think about what's true in my small life,
and of the whole, vast meaning of it all:
Creation, Preservation, and Destruction.
Of how, like epic stories, our own lives—
as the Ganges does, the Colorado, too—
reticulate, flood, fall, fill up again,
and hold and mend from suffering on the way.

Tonight, let lotus blossoms shower down,
to cover my eyes and soothe my tired mind.
I'll wake in my tomorrow's quiet morning
as you head to your bustling, evening market
maze beneath bare bulbs, the bins and stalls
all brimming with bright fruits, exotic vegetables,
and sari silk and dals and wooden crafts,
with spices, breads, gold, baskets, bangles, beads,
dyed and powdered stone for mandalas,
where you'll touch and taste and hear the vital
din of life beneath a purple twilight.

Though our connection has been dropped, I'll say,
as cottonwoods sigh in a western breeze
that through the screen now comes to cool my skin,
I'm here beside you in this moon's blue light,
my love in life, my Sita, my Valmiki.

And I'm there, too, where dawn has just begun
to break in brilliant orange on ancient lands
at the other end of this round world.

Separation

Strange progeny of midnight storm and stone,
one cloud clings to the rocky legs of now,
at dawn, the Wingate pillar *Kissing Couple*
that—earth-bound, mouths locked, eyes closed—weeps in crimson;
what seems to be two solid spires fused
is sandstone being cleft by time and rain.

In gleaming morning as things slowly part,
the sweet aubade of birds is heard which trills
like water flowing still beneath the scree.

Meanwhile over canyons swept and scored,
the cliff-cloud rises into blue, dissolves,
then reappears as something new: It sails

above Mojave, through the Hoh, off Tokyo,
at dusk, a wisp of pink in coral red.

Sedna's Hands

Sedna, Inuit fertility goddess of the sea, is twice betrayed by male figures: first, by a seabird-spirit disguised as a suitor who lures her to his craggy island where he mistreats her; and then by her father who, while rescuing her, is attacked by the indignant seabird's clan. To save himself, he throws Sedna out of his kayak, cutting off her fingers when she tries to climb back in. Defeated, Sedna retreats to the bottom of the sea. Though with reason to be misanthropic, she instead chooses to be benevolent to humankind.

Her wounds are earth's fatal wounds;
no more cat's cradle to fix the sun.
Yet something true lives in the half-lit
world in fading autumn blue
among twisted trees and willow twigs
thin and black, and in the seas
that teem always at the cold top
of the world turning gray and old.
Fertile crimson-green sweeps the air,
the untangling of braided hair.
Her wails have ended.

Her thumbs, the great bow whales, appear
in the leads and wait for us there.
Her fingers swim and fill our nets
to the brim in oblique sunlight.
Walrus, breath steaming, come
streaming to land, with tusks that hold
the draping linen sky, and so
conceals that fearful gaping void.
We hunt, they bleed red on the ice
and feed us in the semi-dark.
She calms.

With face in mangled palms, once hands,
now scarred, cold knobs, she stands
crying as the wild shaman-combing
of her hair sends sparks flying.

They form the circumpolar Bear
who with his siblings of the air
fills the vast, long-lingering night,
bright children she will never bear;
she swallowed raw, false words of one
perfidious pelagic bird.
Still, she remembers

us. Her embers float in the sky
and warm this turning, twilit world,
while she, self-exiled, sits alone
at the dark bottom of the sea.
Though pack ice, turgid, bends and moans,
and rivers, frozen, crack like bones,
in sun or mist, and when it snows,
in open water, on the floes,
everything lives; for, as she chooses,
despite her useless hands, she gives
and gives.

the open window brings inside

the open window brings inside
the sound of water silver
shining in the afternoon
and tree trunks early March are
silver too
and heron skies
are coming back
all blue by rivers tall in thawing marshes

the open window lets them in
our strange ancestors silver
floating in these dusky rooms
and fenceposts in bent grass are
silver too
and owls resurgent
crossing over
thrive in use of now descending shadows

the open window frames in here
the night out there with silver
fragile edges in the night
the moon in every month is
silver too
and cranes and larks
fly into dreams
that tell of change migration stories chance

the window at this moment opens
space for living breathing
in these timeless hours
by the dawn your back is dusted
silver-winged
rising falling
steady still
I close my eyes and I am silver too

IV

Still

Yes, Then I'll Go

Still. Then suddenly the herd is thundering
over plains as one whole formless cloud
that when it meets a yellow hill reticulates
to pounding hot crisscrossing trails of dust
rejoining with wild tumult at the top
where all is gone in one last smoky whorl
that spins, lifts, fades into a boundless blue.

A disappearance I'll make someday, too.

I'll go, go up from this dry August wash
back to the ocean sky and leave behind
this desiccating piece of earth that is
my body-shell.
                But will I ever find
myself beyond that dissolution into—?

For now, I'll take the distance of tomorrow,
the pain of waiting for a quenching rain,
and later leave this lonely, lovely field
whose antelope have fled so recently.

Yes, then I'll go like them, away, away.

On a Northern Shore

The shining neck creates a quivering song. The loon becomes a sound.
Its throat shimmers above the lake, and now the tune becomes a sound.

As the lake takes on night's blank and blackness, all sound is dissolved.
Echoes resound off water, up, and the round moon becomes a sound.

What of those old elegiac notes of dawn's despair? They disappear.
What of desire? With the time to attune, it too becomes a sound.

Sunset once again, and from a silent throat comes something that just *is,*
releasing the long day; that everlasting boon becomes a sound

that washes all away: the light, the water, darkness, and desire.
Wait, pilgrim on the silent shore, listening soon becomes a sound.

To Basho

Birds or leaves?
On this path,
it's hard to tell
what's falling down
from bare, cold branches
or what's flying up to them.

They,
these less-than-concrete
mid-air moments,
matter.
Mid-day or mid-night,
these every shadow moments matter.

Bud and flower;
I see my younger
and my older figure
walking on a crystal road,
moving
to a white and freezing river.

Both
source and mouth
exist at once.
And as the water moves
but freezes,
I stand silently perplexed.

I know what you would say, to only watch
my current feet, hold autumn—now this dying
bird—beneath the rising moon where shadow
limbs and scattered leaves and feathered snow
soothe the ailing earth.

Already

Warm winds abandon earth and fade away
once having lifted life and lain it down
in fields now reaped and waiting for the winter.

Husky stalks, dry, emptied, bend their knees
and lull themselves with whispered songs
of sleep, and with the promise that they lie

upon the meristem of something new.
As dusk descends, day flies and steals the light
and leaves behind bare branches reaching up.

An antlered elk walks to a freezing delta
—braided water green with summer still—
to quench his mind and tangled, fiery veins.

He bellows out his question. Breathing smoke,
he waits stock-still for his autumnal answer.
It comes soon when at the darkened forest

edge, drawn shadows white and dream-like move.

To See the Shining Here

I see their shining auras wild
in yellow fields where snow had been,
new flower heads on tender stems,
all moving in the sun and wind
just after rain from ground that seems
infertile on this rocky stretch,
the rising belly of the West.

Yet I have heard that from thin air
the earth was formed and tilled at dawn,
its fields sown with what beauty is;
the yield desired is not absent—
time and wind and heaving earth
can make deserted places bloom
that we might see the shining here.

The Hills and Hours

Hills in layers. Hills upon the hills
in grays and blues that overlap, broad strokes
of paint. The hum of depth and distance fills
this world of roses, granite, herons, oaks.
>The need for pressed, accustomed places kills
>in time. Nostalgia smolders. Memory smokes.
>Our thoughts drift up, away, and dissipate.
>In quiet kitchens we sit, still, and wait.

The language of the hills is heard in grass,
and spoken, too, by leaves, owls, ferns, and toads.
It's scrawled on streams, wind-etched on lakes of glass,
and found engraved in rock as land erodes.
>And while these living phrases pass
>in lotic, lentic, and tectonic codes
>we might decipher if we'd travel deep,
>we tilt our heads to silent dreams, and sleep.

Palimpsestic—as the old for new gives way—
the hills in folds provide a place to learn
that things emerge as even some decay,
as flames to ashes when the seasons burn.
>Yet we in kitchens of each passing day
>ignore strange landscapes we can't quite discern.
>We sit. And wait. For hours upon the hours,
>flat, still lifes: small vases of cut flowers.

Cranes

One crane in search of his one crane along this braided river
joins the myriad of cranes in grain along this braided river.

They eat in paradise beneath both sun and clouds as shadows
race and, flickering, gild the plain along this braided river.

A cooing throat, a murmuring flute, now herds the scattered flock,
strewn, earthbound, milling in the rain along this braided river.

They meet and wheel and dance on earth, and leap, and slowly fall
with epoch joy, and in refrain along this braided river

sing among the broken stalks to quell their fiery heads,
as trying seeds of doubt remain along this braided river—

reconciliation with the soul's true love is arduous.
But dusk alleviates the strain along this braided river;

behind night's veil, each pairing binds together that one truth
that all their wings and hearts contain along this braided river.

Cranes in blue-dark water marshal for the journey strength
and brace for parting and more pain along this braided river.

At dawn, they rise, and with tremendous booming will, they go.
The husk of sound and need remain along this braided river.

Pilgrim, go with cranes, and with their light and feathers fly.
Leave behind your body-brain along this braided river.

Night Verses

The airy rush of thoughts today
the evening breeze has whisked away.

The wind that spoke to me in wings
has flown and left old, scattered things.

Some small and faint discarded words
remain like fragile bones of birds.

I gather letters from the ground,
recall their lofty flight and sound

and turn their verses rune by rune
to lines beneath the harvest moon.

Revived, deciphered bird I know
I'll hold a moment, then let go.

About the Author

Brian Palmer was raised in the Midwest and has since lived for much of his life in the various and singular regions of Colorado with some intervening years in the Pacific Northwest. Each of these places—with its unique topography, natural beauty, history, and spirit—has and continues to significantly affect his life and poetry. After a fulfilling career as a high school English teacher and theater director, he now pursues full-time his interests in reading, studying, and writing poetry. He publishes his work regularly in various print and on-line journals, and he's the editor of *THINK: A Journal of Poetry, Fiction, and Essays*. He currently lives in Juneau, Alaska.

www.ingramcontent.com/pod-product-compliance
Lightning Source LLC
Chambersburg PA
CBHW031205160426
43193CB00008B/512